Mel Bay presents

DADGAD
Chords, Scales, and Tuning

by Felix Schell

Pages 2 and 39 are left blank intentionally

1 2 3 4 5 6 7 8 9 0

© 2002 BY MEL BAY PUBLICATIONS, INC., PACIFIC, MO 63069.

Visit us on the Web at www.melbay.com — E-mail us at email@melbay.com

Contents

Preface

This book offers a large number of essential chords and scales for the DADGAD tuning of the guitar. The material assembled here opens up a multitude of possibilities to expand and improve your playing in this unique tuning. It made sense to me to show these chords in their customary harmonic contexts, instead of just listing them (as is done in most straight forward chord-books). Skim and skip to taste, experiment, and linger where ever you find your musical inspiration. Have fun with this new, unique DADGAD book.

Felix Schell

How to tune the guitar into DADGAD

The DADGAD tuning can be derived from the standard tuning of the guitar (EADGBD) in the following manner:

1. Tune the sixth string (low E) down by a whole tone to D. To do this, refer to the pitch of the 4th string (D), which sounds one octave higher.

2. The tuning of the 5th, 4th, and 3rd string (A,D,and G) remain unchanged.

3. Tune the 2nd string (B) down by a whole tone to A. Refer to the pitch of the 5th string (A), which sounds one octave lower.

4. Tune the 1st string (E) down by a whole tone to D. To do this, compare it's sound to the sound of the 4th (sounds one octave lower) and 6th string (sounds two octaves lower).

Regular Tuning	E	A	D	g	b	e
to	one step lower	same note	same note	same note	one step lower	one step lower
DADGAD -Tuning	D	A	D	g	a	d

General Explanations

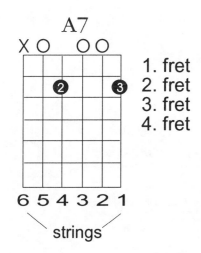

A7

1. fret
2. fret
3. fret
4. fret

6 5 4 3 2 1
strings

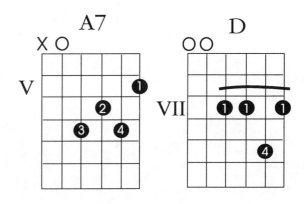

A7   D

4   indicates which finger to use and which fret to place it on

O   open string

X   muted or not played string

VII   roman numbers represent the frets

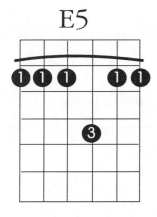

E5

Barre chords are moveable !

Barre chords can be played on each fret of the entire fingerboard. Therefore you get 11 additional chords for each chord shown. In order to name the chord, you need to know the notes of the chromatic scale. The chromatic scale is made up entirely from consecutive half tone steps. A half tone step corresponds to the movement from one fret of the guitar to the next . These are the names of the notes of the chromatic scale: C, C♯, D, D♯, E, F, F♯, G, G♯, A, A♯, B.
After this the scale repeats itself one octave higher. The E5 chord on the left is located on the 2nd fret. Move it up to the 3rd fret, and you will get an F5 chord. Played on the 4th fret it will be F♯5, on the 5th fret G5 and so on.
Non-barre chords are moveable as well. The open strings have to be taken into consideration, though. These can only be played if they are part of the chord (Root, third, fifth or an extension).

Scales

The following text shows the fingering of different scales. The respective roots are indicated by a box.

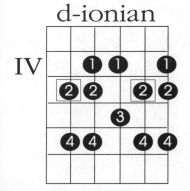

d-ionian

IV

Chapter 1
Key of D Major

chords:	D	Em	F#m	G	A	Bm	C#°
scale degrees:	I	ii	iii	IV	V	vi	vii

The harmonized major scale

I (1st chord, also refered to as the tonic)
D major is the tonic in the key of D major. This chord can have the following extensions: maj7, 6, 6/9, 5, maj7/9, maj13.

ii (2nd chord)
Em is a substitute for G major. This chord can have the following extensions: m7, m9, m11.

iii (3rd chord)
F#m is a substitute for A major. F#m can have the same extensions as the ii. chord: m7, m9, m11.

IV (4th chord, also refered to as the subdominant)
G major is the subdominant in the key of D major. This chord can have the same extensions as the 1. chord: maj7, 6, 6/9, 5, maj7/9, maj13.

V (5th chord, also refered to as the dominant)
A major is the dominant in the key of D major. This chord can have the following extensions: 7, 7/9, 11, 13, 7♭9, 7#9, 7♭5, 7#5, sus4.

vi (6th chord)
Bm is a substitude for D major. Bm can have the same extensions as the ii and iii chord.

The label "no 3rd" means: This chord does not contain the 3rd.

The label "no 7" means: This extended chord does not contain a seventh.

Key of D Major
Chord Progression V - I
Dominant - Tonic
A7 - D

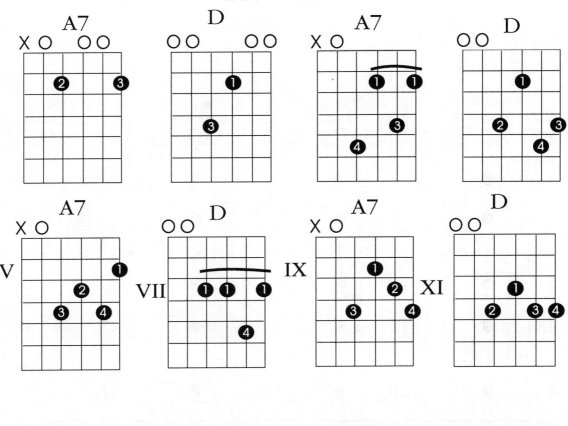

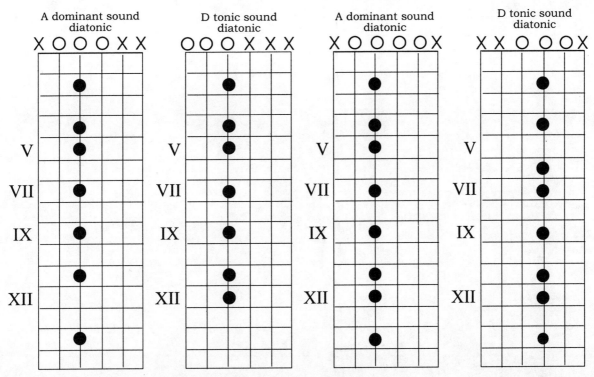

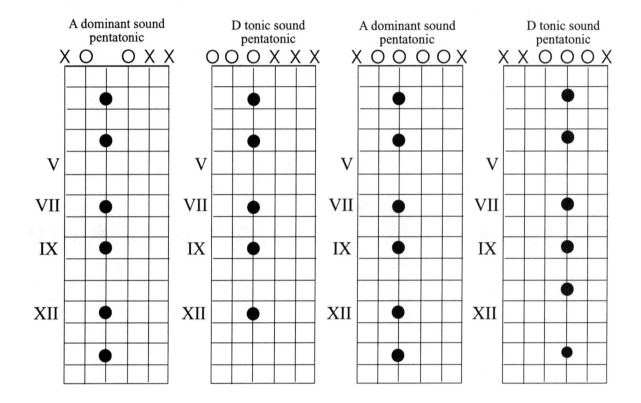

Chord Progression
Vsus4 - V - I
Dominant/ sus4 - Dominant - Tonic
Asus4 - A - D

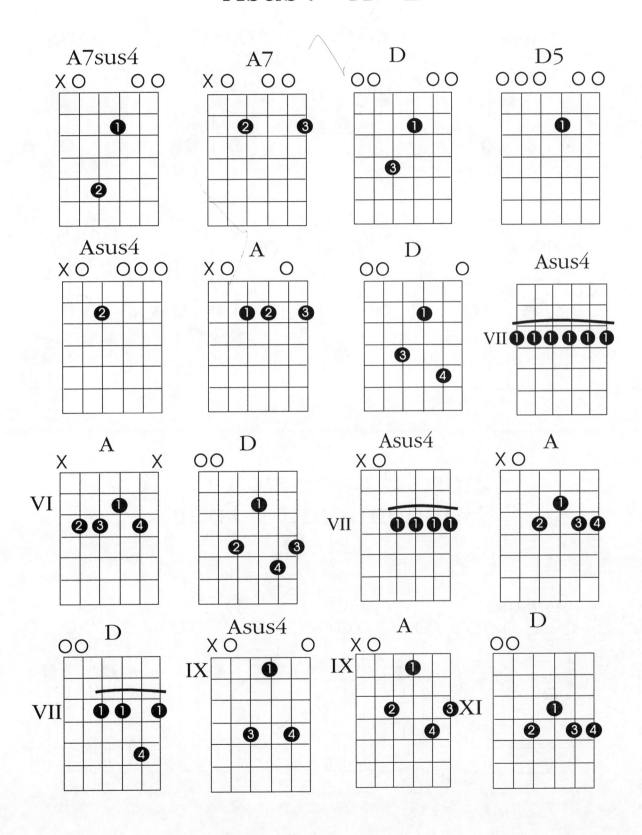

Chord Progression I - IV
Tonic - Subdominant
D - G

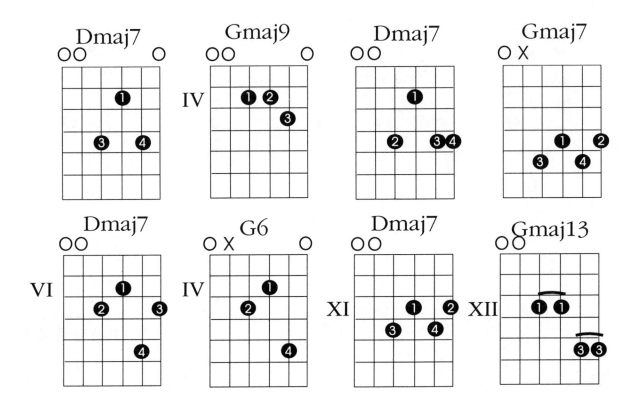

Chord Progression IV - I
Subdominant - Tonic
G - D

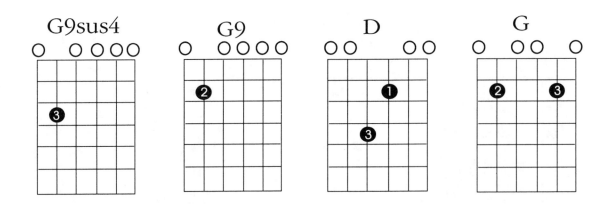

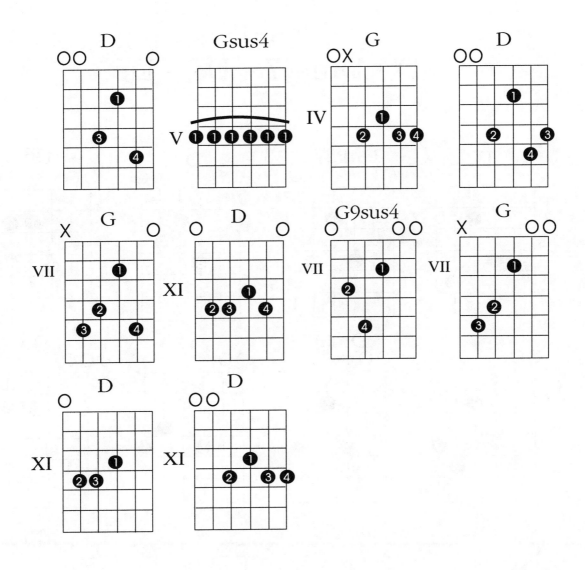

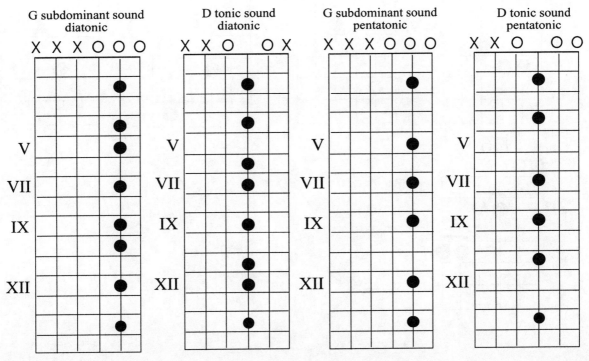

G subdominant sound
diatonic

D tonic sound
diatonic

G subdominant sound
pentatonic

D tonic sound
pentatonic

Line Progression I - Imaj7 - I7 - I6
Tonic
D - Dmaj7 - D7 - D6

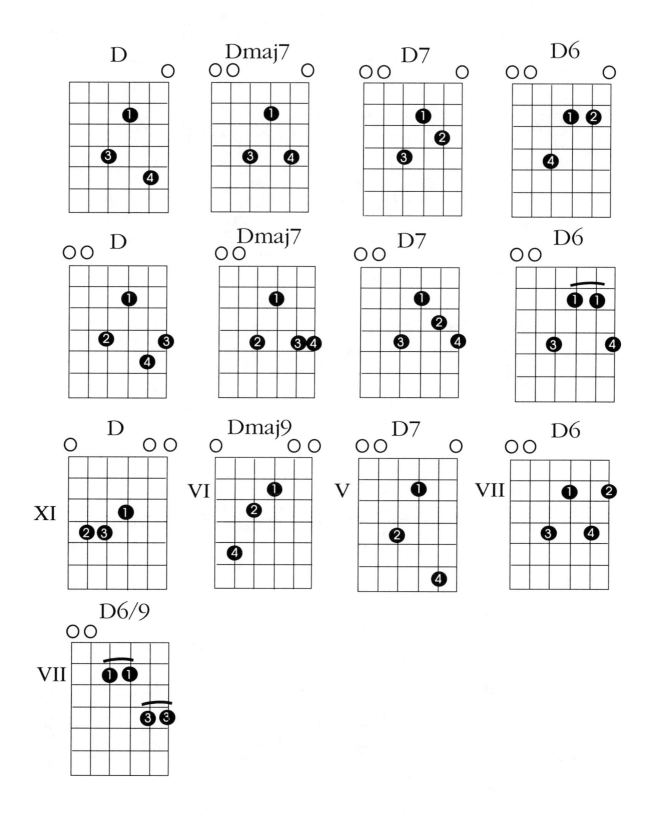

D Major Scale (Diatonic)
D E F♯ G A B C♯

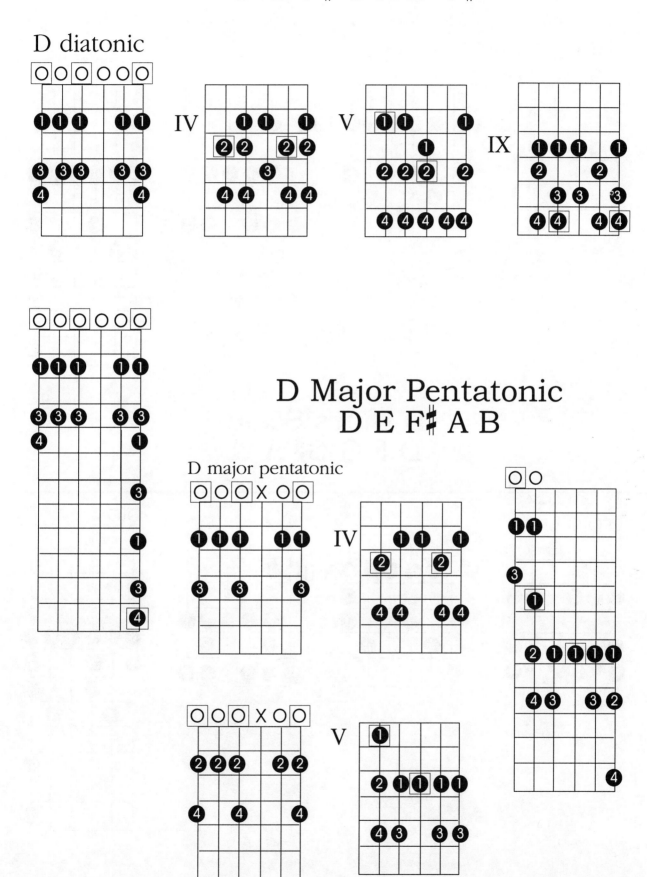

D Major Pentatonic
D E F♯ A B

D Minor Pentatonic
D F G A C

D minor pentatonic

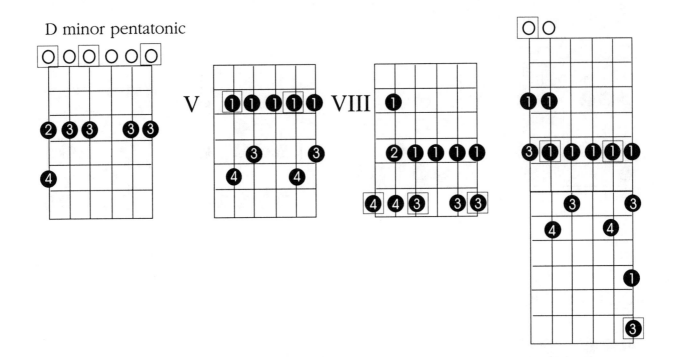

D Blues Scale
D F G G♯ A C

D blues scale

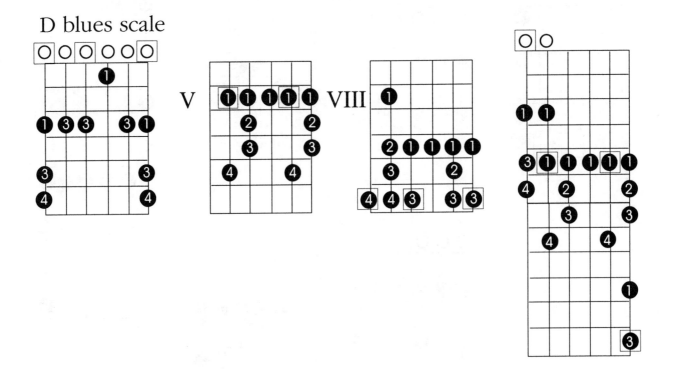

14

I - IV - V - I (D Minor)

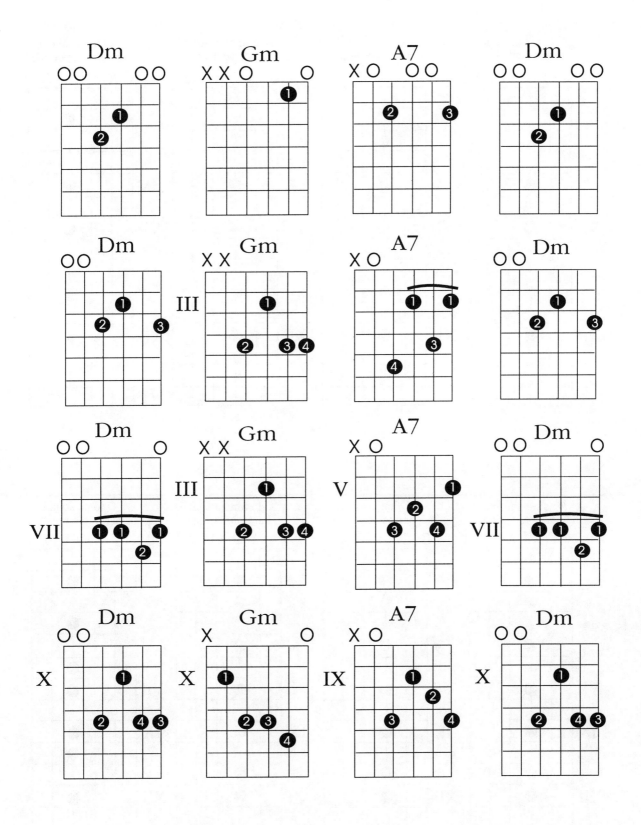

15

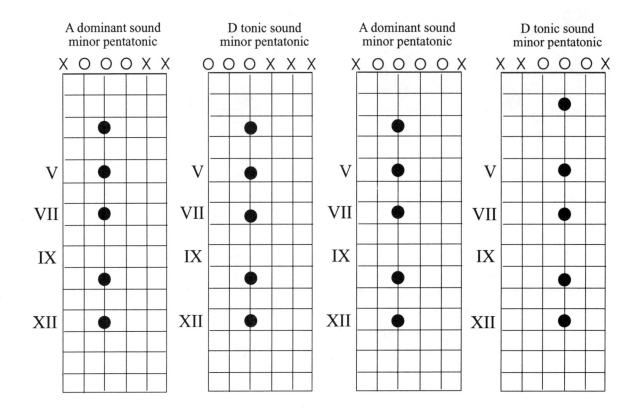

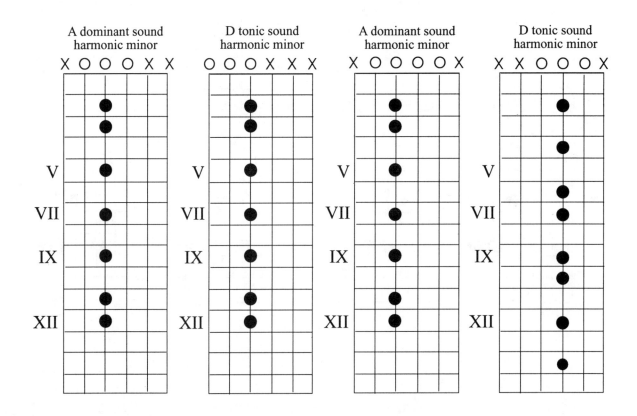

D Minor Scale (Natural Minor, Aeolian)
D E F G A B♭ C

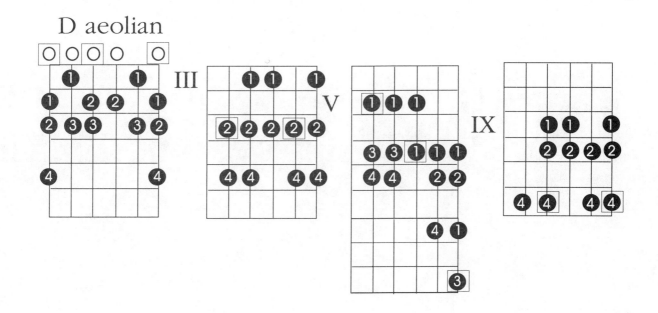

D Harmonic Minor Scale
D E F G A B♭ C♯

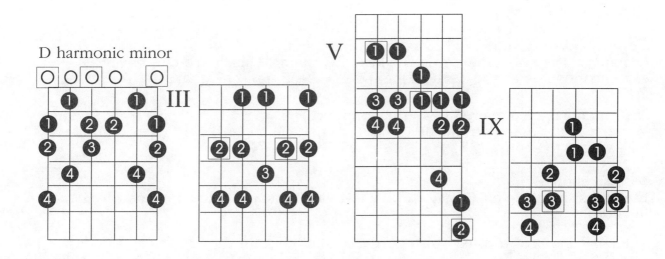

17

Chapter 2
Key of G major

chords:	G	Am	Bm	C	D	Em	F♯^o
scale degrees:	I	ii	iii	IV	V	vi	vii

The harmonized major scale

I (1st chord, also refered to as the tonic)
G major is the tonic in the key of G major. This chord can have the following extensions: maj7, 6, 6/9, 5, maj7/9, maj13.

ii (2nd chord)
Am is a substitute for C major. This chord can have the following extensions: m7, m9, m11.

iii (3rd chord)
Bm is a substitute for D major. Bm can have the same extensions as the ii. chord: m7, m9, m11.

IV (4th chord, also refered to as the subdominant)
C major is the subdominant in the key of G major. This chord can have the same extensions as the 1. chord: maj7, 6, 6/9, 5, maj7/9, maj13.

V (5th chord, also refered to as the dominant)
D major is the dominant in the key of G major. This chord can have the following extensions: 7, 7/9, 11, 13, 7♭9, 7♯9, 7♭5, 7♯5, sus4.

vi (6th chord)
Em is a substitude for G major. Bm can have the same extensions as the ii and iii chord.

The label "no 3rd" means: This chord does not contain the 3rd.

The label "no 7" means: This extended chord does not contain a seventh.

Key of G Major
Chord Progression V - I
Dominant - Tonic
D - G

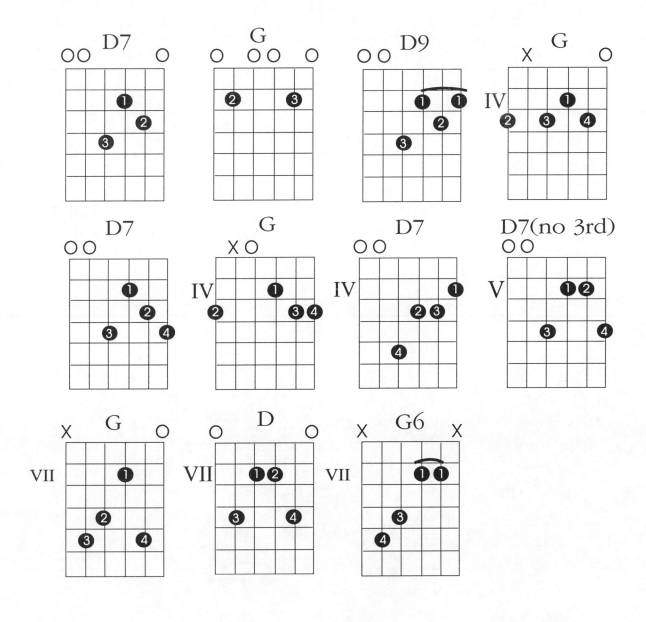

Chord Progression
Vsus4-V-I
Dominant/ sus4 - Dominant - Tonic
Dsus4-D-G

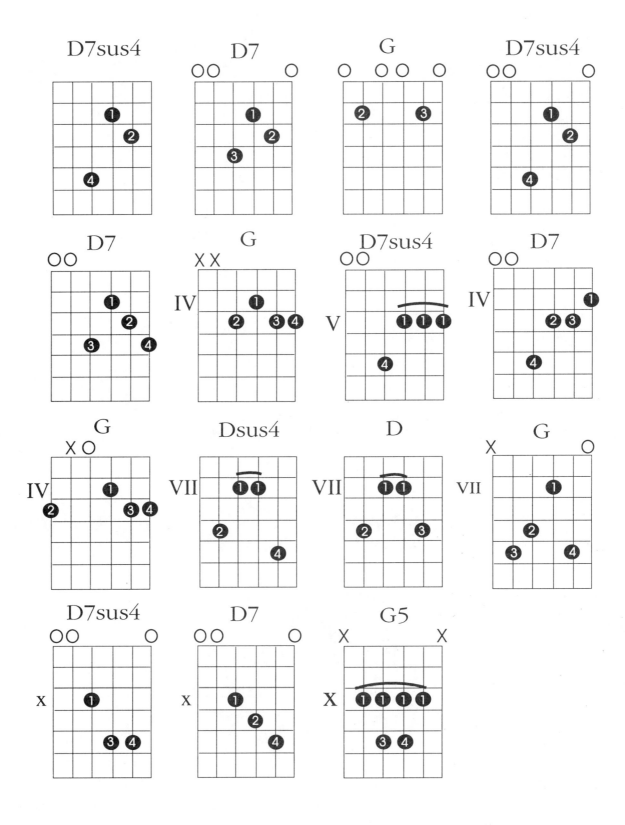

Chord Progression I - IV
Tonic - Subdominant
G - C

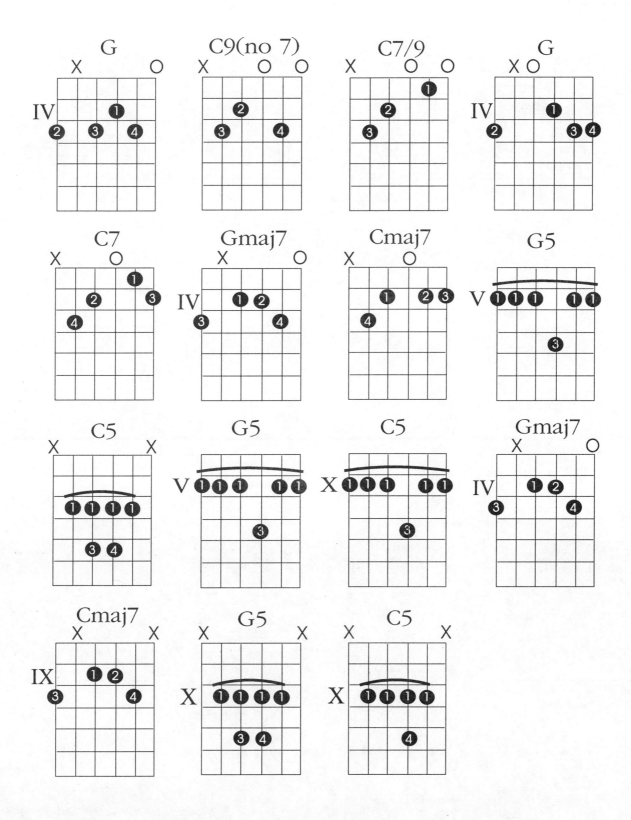

Chord Progression II - V
Substitute Of The Subdominant - Dominant
Am - D

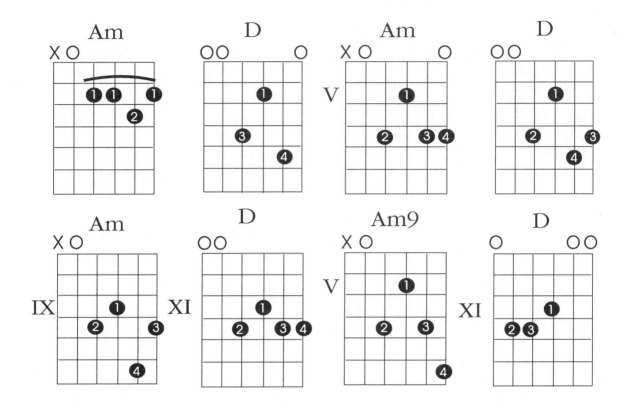

22

II - IIm#7 - IIm7 - V

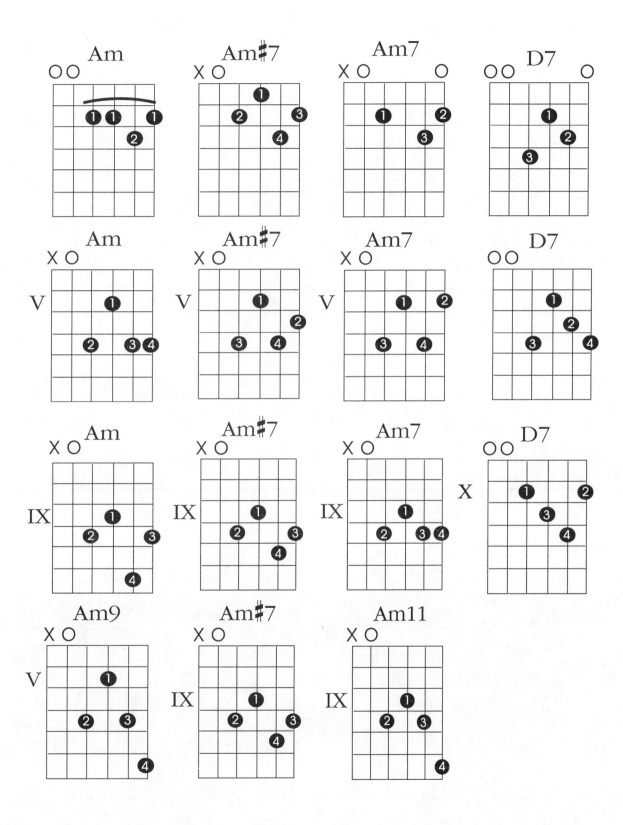

Chord Progression I - Imaj7 - I7 - IV
Tonic - Subdominant
G - Gmaj7 - G7 - C

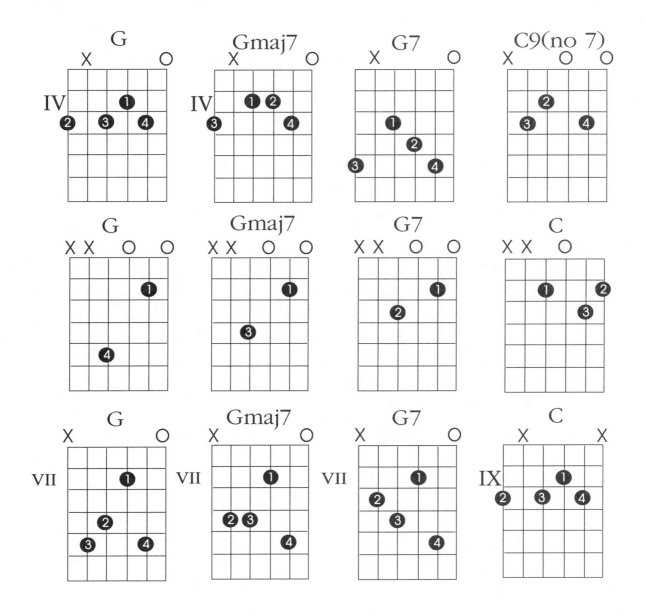

G Major Scale (Diatonic)
G A B C D E F♯

G diatonic

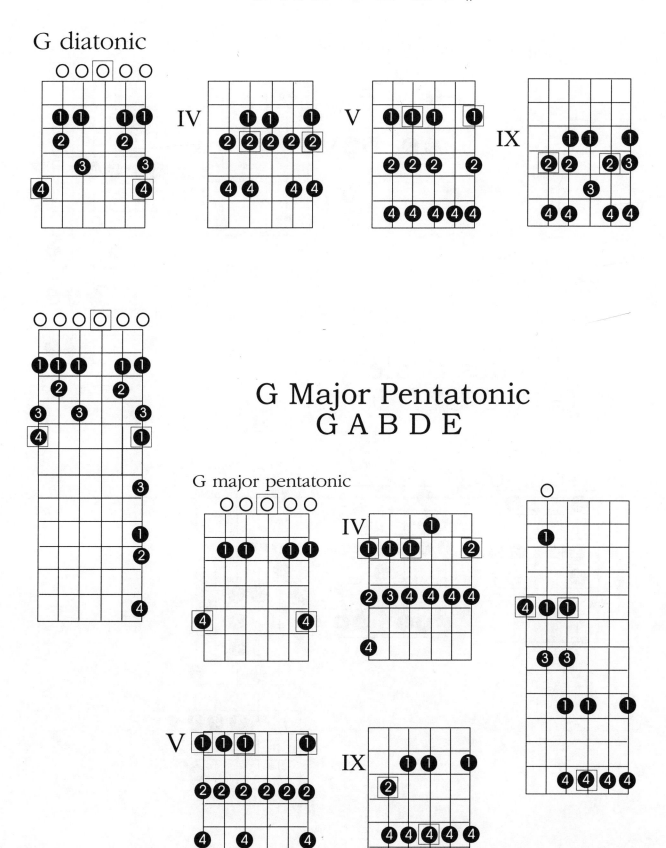

G Major Pentatonic
G A B D E

G major pentatonic

25

G Minor Pentatonic
G B♭ C D F

G minor pentatonic

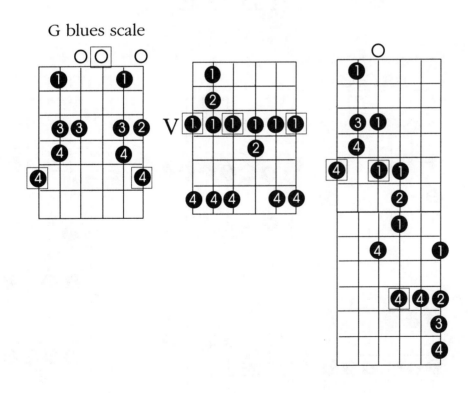

G Blues Scale
G B♭ C C♯ D F

G blues scale

Chapter 2
Key of A Major

chords:	A	Bm	C#m	D	E	F#m	G#°
scale degrees:	I	ii	iii	IV	V	vi	vii

The harmonized major scale

I (1st chord, also refered to as the tonic)
A major is the tonic in the key of A major. This chord can have the following extensions: maj7, 6, 6/9, 5, maj7/9, maj13.

ii (2nd chord)
Bm is a substitute for D major. This chord can have the following extensions: m7, m9, m11.

iii (3rd chord)
C#m is a substitude for E major. C#m can have the same extensions as the ii. chord: m7, m9, m11.

IV (4th chord, also refered to as the subdominant)
D major is the subdominant in the key of A major. This chord can have the same extensions as the 1. chord: maj7, 6, 6/9, 5, maj7/9, maj13.

V (5th chord, also refered to as the dominant)
E major is the dominant in the key of A major. This chord can have the following extensions: 7, 7/9, 11, 13, 7b9, 7#9, 7b5, 7#5, sus4.

vi (6th chord)
F#m is a substitute for A major. Bm can have the same extensions as the ii and iii chord.

The label "no 3rd" means: This chord does not contain the 3rd.

The label "no 7" means: This extended chord does not contain a seventh.

Key of A Major
Chord Progression V - I
Dominant - Tonic
E - A

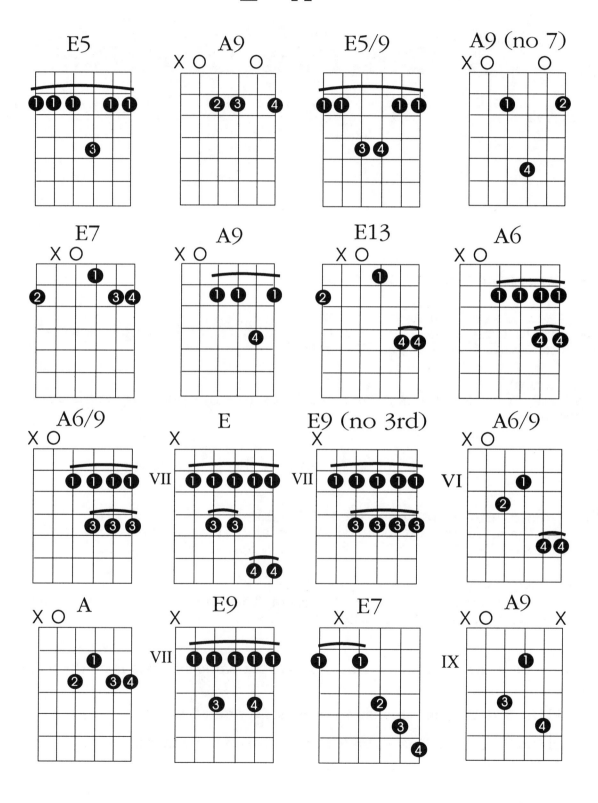

Chord Progression
Vsus4 - V - I
Dominant/sus4 - Dominant - Tonic
Esus4 - E - A

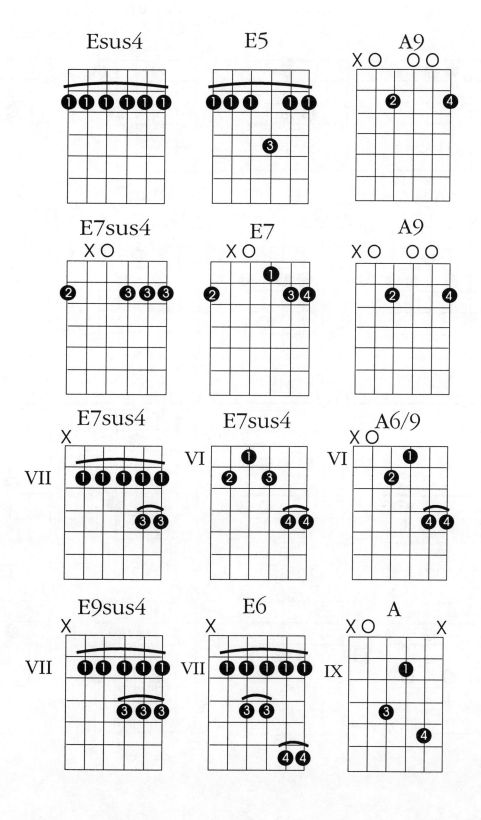

Chord Progression I - IV
Tonic - Subdominant
A - D

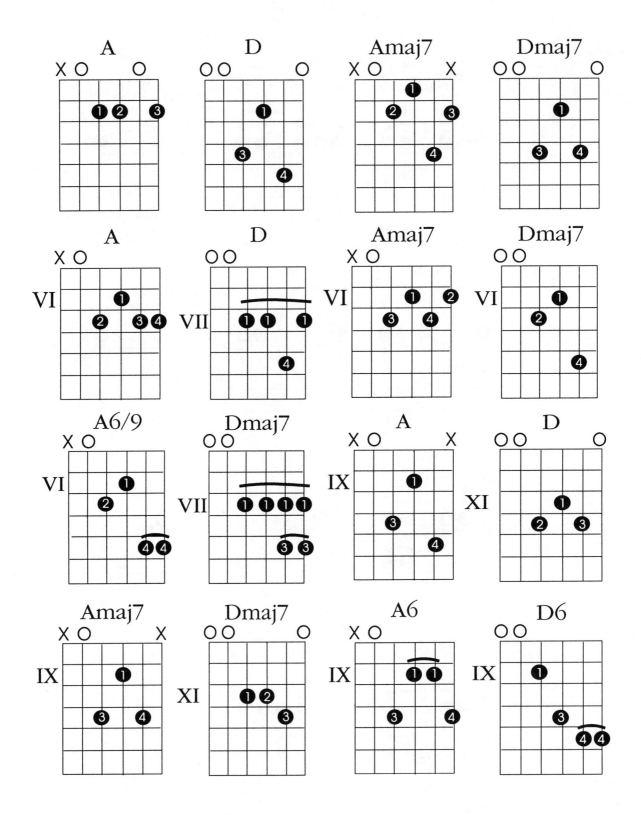

Chord Progression II - V
Substitute Of The Subdominant - Dominant
Bm - E

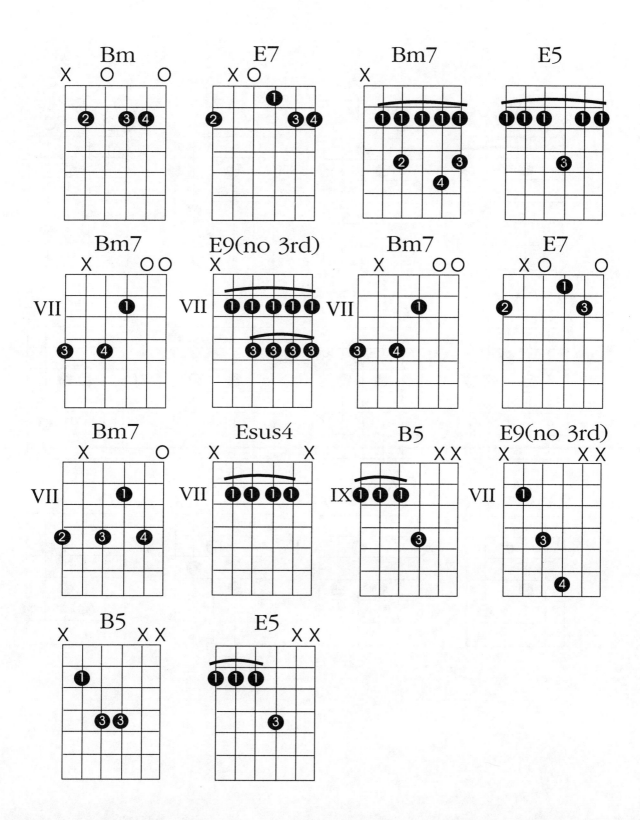

Chord Progression I - Imaj7 - I7 - IV
Tonic - Subdominant
A - Amaj7 - A7 - D

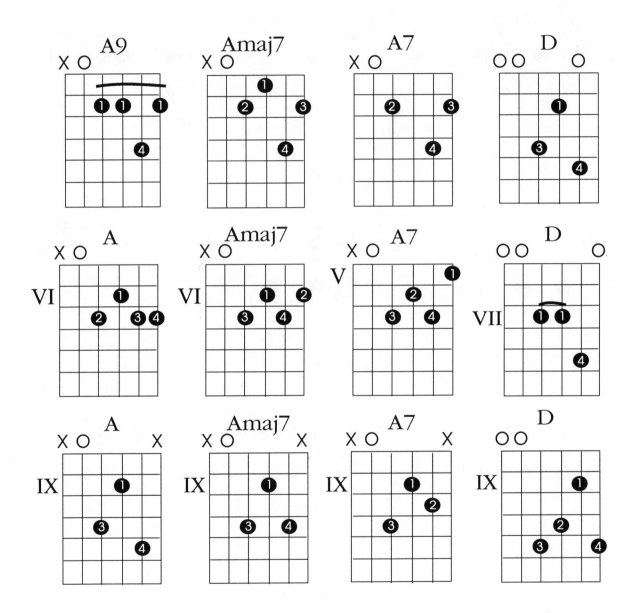

A Major Scale (Diatonic)
A B C♯ D E F♯ G♯

A diatonic

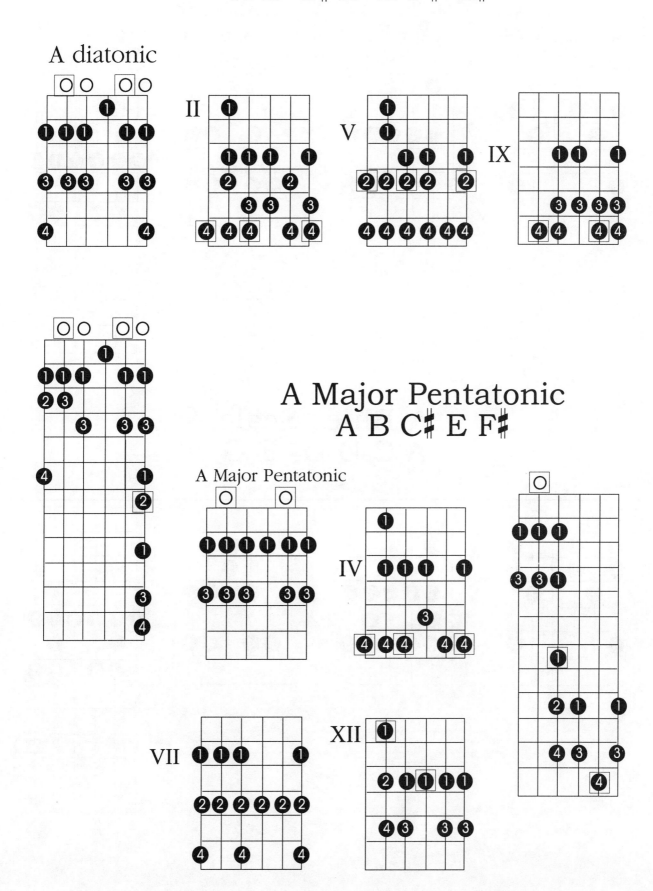

A Major Pentatonic
A B C♯ E F♯

A Major Pentatonic

A Minor Pentatonic
A C D E G

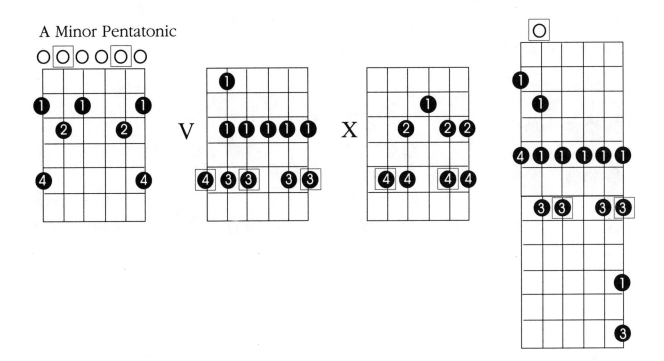

A-Blues Scale
A C D D♯ E G

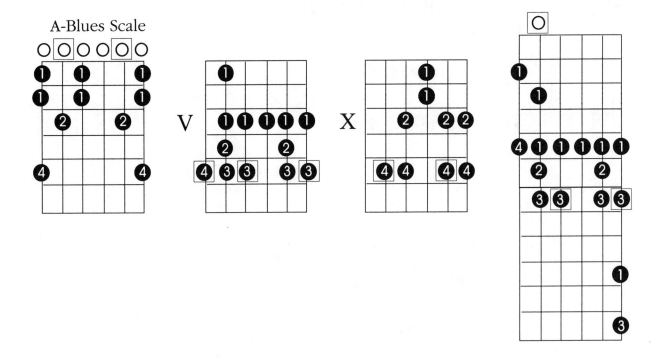

Key of C-Major
Chord Progression II - V
Substitude Of The Subdominant - Dominant
Dm - G

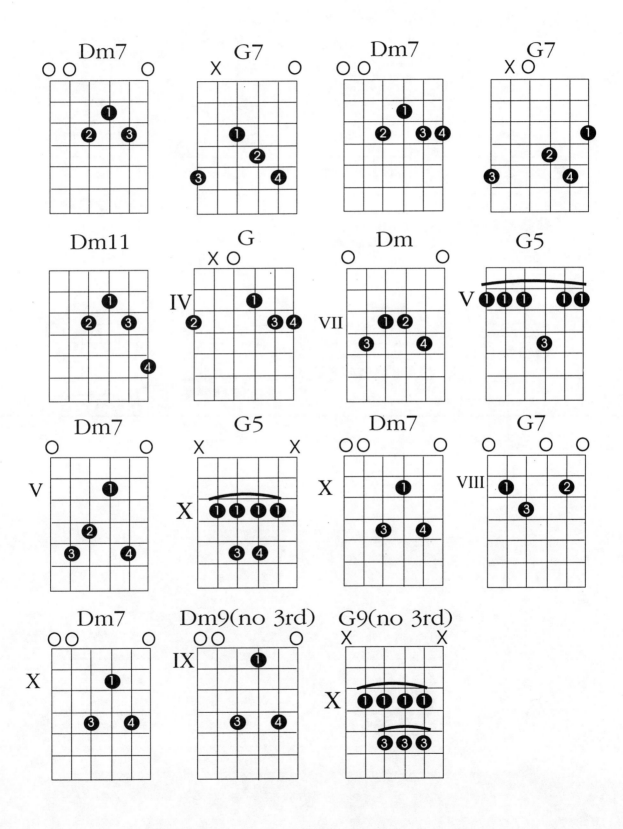

Special Chords

sus4, 5, (a chord containing no third, also called "Power Chord")
diminished, augmented

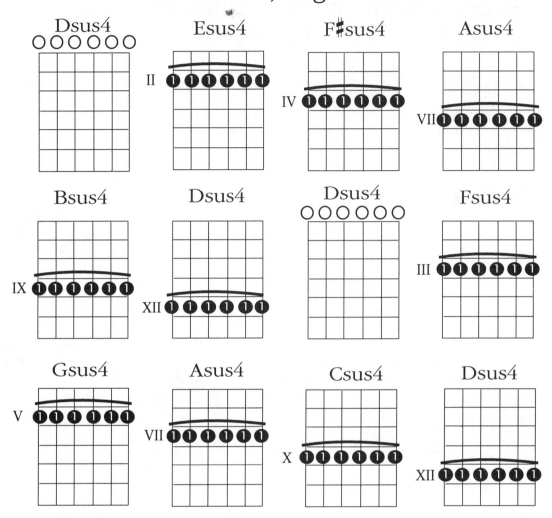

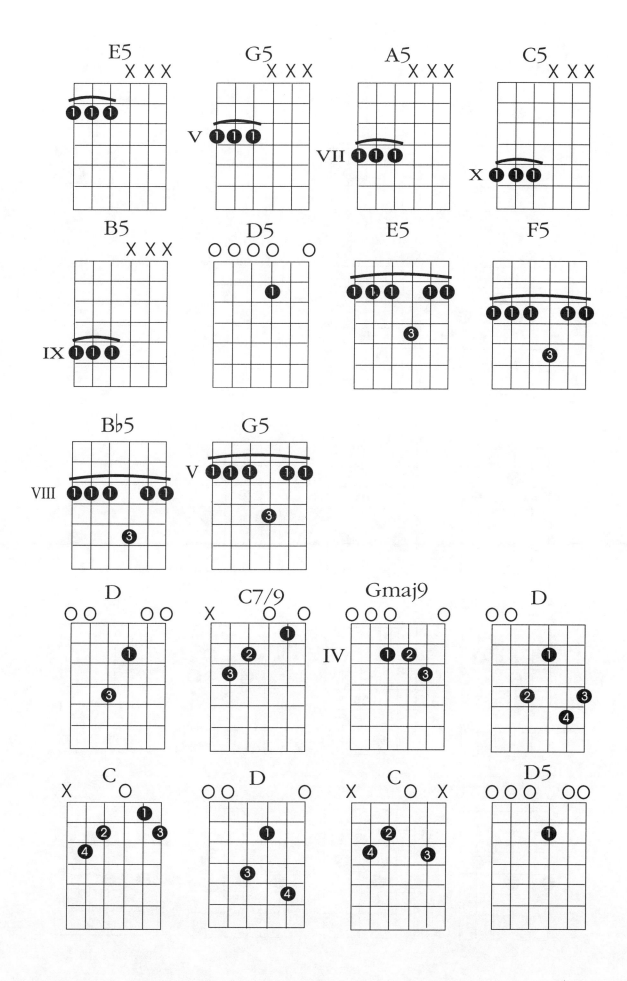

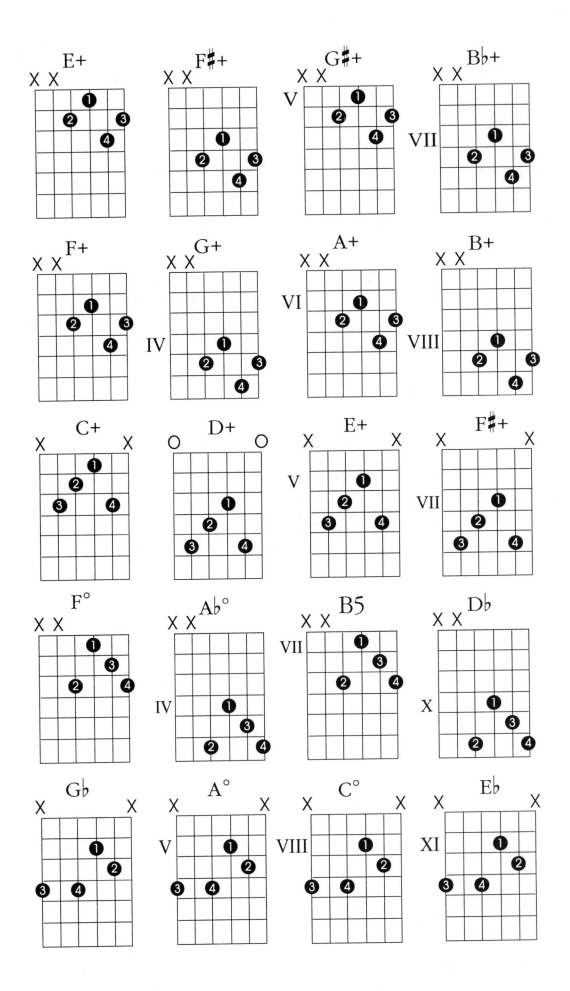

38